A BOOT UP

THE BLACKDOWN HILLS

Rodney Legg

First published in Great Britain in 2009

British Library Cataloguing-in-Publication Data
A CIP record for this title is available from the British Library

ISBN 978 1 906887 22 3

PiXZ Books
Halsgrove House, Ryelands Industrial Estate,
Bagley Road, Wellington, Somerset TA21 9PZ
Tel: 01823 653777
Fax: 01823 216796
email: sales@halsgrove.com

An imprint of Halstar Ltd, part of the Halsgrove group of companies
Information on all Halsgrove titles is available at: www.halsgrove.com

Printed and bound by Grafiche Flaminia, Italy

Contents

The Blackdowns

How to use this book

The Area

'I'm off to the Blackdown Hills' usually receives a one-word response: 'Where?' They remain a well-kept secret. Though straddling the central boundaries of Devon and Somerset the area is unknown to many in each county. Despite being crossed in the south by the A30, the A303 and the A35, much of the area is truly remote. It more than justifies designation as an area of outstanding natural beauty though official confirmation of this was a long time coming.

Johnny Cash recorded an Irish song that also sums up the Blackdowns: 'Forty shades of green.' This is a lush landscape that can be pure Ireland in its colour chart values for shades of green, from virtual yellows in spring through to what printers

identify as PMS 5535 (for the rest of us synonymous with the National Trust). All shades are liable to come with fluorescent gradations and overlays from a painter's light that is the inland answer to St Ives.

Underfoot, in walking terms, you pay the price. Between the flat-topped ridges, steep slopes and squelchy springs are the norm. Flint-like cherts sit on a bed of greensand and clay in an area of high rainfall that is often under a cloud. So mud is always liable to be on the menu and you will inevitably slip and slide. Dress accordingly.

Another twist to the Blackdowns is that apart from where you can see the Wellington Monument, or Stockland Hill transmitter, there is a distinct shortage of landmarks. Pastures, plateaus, valleys and woods often look much the same. This can

make walking mentally as well as physically strenuous. You may well need to use that compass – particularly if the Sun isn't shining – if only for reassurance that you are heading the right way.

Expect a shortage of buses, cafés and public houses though for the latter there are a few strategically-placed exceptions such as Culm Valley Inn, the Holman Clavel, the Merry Harriers and the Sidmouth Arms, without having to retreat to the A303 roadhouse which is the Eagle Tavern. Despite these reservations you will find superb walking country across the Blackdown Hills.

The Routes

All routes are circular – meaning they bring you back to the starting point – and are of moderate length. They vary from four to nine miles and are graded from one to three boots — from easy to the more challenging. They are ideal for families or groups of friends looking for an afternoon in glorious historic countryside or for a more leisurely walk with a suitable pause at a pub or refreshment spot en route. None of the terrain is pushchair friendly, so back-pack the toddler.

Starting points are given with map references and postcodes, because the latter are necessary for some car-borne navigation systems, including that used by an ambulance crew who told me they were 15 minutes late in arriving at an emergency because no postcode was given.

Direction details specify compass points which, clockwise, are N (north), NNE (north-northeast), E (east), ESE (east-southeast), SE (south-east), SSE (south-southeast), S (south), SSW (south-southwest), SW (south-west), WSW (west-southwest), W (west), WNW (west-northwest), NW (north-west) and WNW (west-northwest). The general direction can be assumed to remain the same until another compass point is given. Carry a compass.

Routes are along public rights of way or across access land. Both categories may be subject to change or diversion. Remember that conditions under foot will vary greatly according to the season and the weather. Do not set off into the hills if fog is likely.

Parking spaces are specified on the assumption that many walkers will arrive by car or bicycle. Where public transport is mentioned, there were options currently available, but check these with the provider before setting off and always make sure you also know the time of the last bus or train.

Maps

Though we give a self-contained potted description of each walk you may need a map or global positioning system to find its parking point. Our sketch maps can only be a rough guide. A detailed map will prove useful if you stray away from the route or are forced to cut the walk short. Remember that practical difficulties on the day may range from heat exhaustion to hill fog.

The Blackdown Hills are awkwardly placed, as far as the Ordnance Survey is concerned, across three large-scale sheets. The northern half currently appears on two sides of Explorer Map 128 (Taunton & Blackdown Hills). The southern half is split between Explorer Map 115 (Exmouth and Sidmouth) for Honiton district and Explorer Map 116 (Lyme Regis & Bridport) to cover the Chard area. For availability access www.ordnancesurvey.co.uk/leisure.

Key to Symbols Used

Level of difficulty:

Easy 🍃
Moderate 🍃🍃
More Challenging 🍃🍃🍃

Map symbols:

🚗	Park & start
────	Tarred Road
– – –	Footpath
– – –	Walk Footpath
■	Building
+	Church
▲	Triangulation pillar or other landmark
🚻	WC
🍴	Refreshments
🪣	Pub

Walk Locations

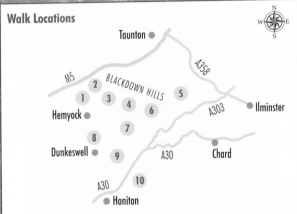

Taunton

M5   BLACKDOWN HILLS

A358

Hemyock

1 2 3 4 5 6

7

8

Dunkeswell

9

A303   Ilminster

A30   Chard

10

A30

Honiton

1 Culm Davy and Black Down

An iconic 5-mile circuit of the great plateau that gives its name to these hills.

Crossways Farm

Higher Wrangway

1

BLACK DOWN COMMON

Mast

12

Keeper's Cottage

11

WHITEHALL PLANTATION

CULM DAVY PLANTATION

CLEMENT'S COMMON

10

2

stock acon

9

8

Culm Davy

7

Pithayne Farm

3

6

5

4

Scale ⌞ 500m ⌟

Having an Elizabethan beacon tops off Black Down's claims as a great, open unenclosed landscape that has hardly changed in centuries. It is the Black Down of the Blackdown Hills with one of the largest tracts of common land. This is wild now but was previously used both for quarrying gravel and as a racecourse. Beneath it lies Culmstock, with a chunky mediaeval bridge beside Culm Valley Inn, which used to be the Railway Inn. Culmstock Station was on a cul-de-sac line into the valley from Tiverton Junction to a milk factory at Hemyock.

Level: ♥ ♥
Length: 5 miles
Terrain: One long climb but otherwise easy going.
Park & start: On the roadside verge west of the hairpin bend above Wrangway, towards the bend, beside the track to Crossways Farm at Higher Wrangway.
Start ref: ST 127 167
Postcode: TA21 9QH
Public transport: None
Websites:
www.blackdown.hills.net
www.ukvillages.co.uk/village/culm

It opened on 29 May 1876 and closed just short of its centenary on 3 November 1975.

① Set off (E) back to the main corner in 300 metres and turn right (S) towards Culmstock. The pine plantations and older woodland of Culm Davy Forest, to the right, are access land which you can enter, to Keeper's Cottage in 600 metres. Proceed to the Blackaller junction in another 500 metres. Continue to the corner in 250 metres.

② Turn right (SW) into the double-hedge green lane which looks down to the left over Hemyock. In 300 metres we come to a cottage and a lane. Turn left (S) down to the junction in 150 metres.

③ Turn right (SW) and then right again in just 5 metres (but for a diversion to see Culm Davy Church

Culmstock Beacon.

continue downhill to Chapel Farm and then return to the double corners). Our onward lane is through Cotlands hamlet.

④ Turn right (W) in 400 metres, into the second farm track, which is 'Unsuitable for motors'.

Devon's Black Down Common, which merges seamlessly with Somerset's Sampford Common, provides the generic name for the Blackdown Hills.

Today's beacon.

Fire-buckets in the stone igloo-shaped Culmstock Beacon sent warning to London of the Spanish Armada in 1588.

 Turn left at the end in 600 metres, into the lane, and go round two corners. Turn right (SW) at the triangle of grass in 200 metres, into a double-hedged green lane.

In 400 metres we come to Pithayne Farm. Turn right (N) through the two gates to the right of the farmhouse, to head into the hills. A short stub of green lane leads into two fields in 150 metres. Proceed straight ahead across the lower corner of the first field and then into the second field in 30 metres.

Culmstock slopes.

Black Down Common.

Representing the local populace, the Lutleys occupy the biggest corner of Culm Davy churchyard, and descendant Wendy Lutley is still going strong, running Folk South-West and campaigning against a new road through the Blackdowns.

(7) Follow its hedgerow (NW) and keep it to your right. The valley opens up to the left and the bracken-clad slope of Culmstock Beacon arises ahead. Cross the stile and follow the old hedge, climbing gradually to the wild land at the end of the pastures, in 350 metres.

(8) Here we go through the gate and follow the hedge at the lower end of the slope. Turn right in 125 metres, to find a path that heads diagonally up the hillside, through the bracken. In 200 metres this brings us to the fence-line with the pasture where we turn left for the last 50 metres of the climb.

(9) Turn left on joining the hilltop track, to the Elizabethan stone bee-hive shaped Culmstock Beacon in 200 metres. Positioned at 820 feet above sea level, it has slits looking towards beacon sites at Upottery and Holcombe Rogus, and the door faces the main line of the Blackdown Hills.

Culm Davy Church.

Cotlands.

10 Turn right (N), passing the Ordnance Survey triangulation pillar, and follow the gravel track for 750 metres. Turn right (NE) on reaching the next gravel track – a bridleway – and climb on to the main expanse of Black Down Common. Down to the left, across a patchwork of green fields, runs the M5 from Devon into Somerset.

Well-heeled graves at Culm Davy include the 1st Baron Bateman, Sir John Follett, the Gervis family who adopted Bournemouth, and Lieutenant-Colonel Henry Green-Wilkinson.

(11) Continue straight ahead, by effectively forking left, in 700 metres. The bridleway takes the right-hand fork but our route across access land is a big grassy loop of 900 metres which formed the major part of a Victorian racecourse. There is a communications mast to the right and the grassy strip eventually turns towards it. Then we follow the path towards trees to the right of the mast.

Lieutenant-Colonel Peter Dobree gave the Beacon and its surrounding 60 acres to the people of Culmstock in 1995, to create a nature reserve for nesting nightjars, stonechats and Dartford warblers.

Pithayne primroses.

Rhubarb pots.

(12) Rejoin the hilltop bridleway and turn left along it. Go through the gate into a wide and muddy track beside the conifers of Whitehall Plantation which is also access land. Broomfield Breach, a fenced area of rough ground, is to the left. In 250 metres we pass the mast and follow its access road down to Crossways Farm in 400 metres. Continue straight ahead to return to your car in 150 metres.

2 **Wellington Monument and Quarts Moor**

Monument-based 4-mile circuit of the wooded 900-feet toplands and its slopes.

The Wellington Monument is synonymous with the Blackdown Hills. The landmark that is shared with drivers on the M5 motorway. It represents a direct link with the Anglo-Irish victor of Waterloo who adopted the name of the Somerset town for his dukedom though he visited just once. Three areas of conservation land are crossed en route. There is also a Wellingtonia — the great American redwood named in honour of the Iron Duke — in the vale at Legglands. The views are northwards over Taunton Deane to the Brendon Hills, Quantock Hills and the Bristol Channel. South Wales forms the distant horizon on a clear day.

Map labels:
Legglands
Calway's Farm
6
7
4
5
8
Briscoe
Voxmoor
9
3
Beacon Lane Farm
Quarts Farm
2
FIRS PLANTATION
QUARTS MOOR
lington nument
Monument Road
10
1
11
12
Hemyock Place

Scale 500m

Level: ♥♥
Length: 4 miles
Terrain: Marshy in places with a long, stony climb.
Park & start: In the National Trust car park for the Wellington Monument, above Wellington.
Start ref: ST 144 167
Postcode: TA21 9PB
Public transport: Buses from Wellington to Hemyock.
Websites:
www.tauntondeane.gov.uk
www.wellington.somerset.com

Wellington Monument.

The tallest triangular obelisk in the world commemorates Field-Marshal Arthur Wellesley, 1st Duke of Wellington (1769–1852), the victor of the French Wars, who was bodily towed in his carriage to visit this viewpoint in 1819.

The foundations for the 175-feet high Wellington Monument, on a former beacon site, were laid in 1817 but it remained unfinished when the Iron Duke died in 1852 and was not 'topped out' until 1892.

1 Set off along the track (NW), through the barrier, to the Wellington Monument in 800 metres.

2 Turn right (NE) behind the obelisk, from the topograph, down a flight of steps into the wood. Drop down to a National Trust sign and cross the stile under the beech trees. Bear right across the spring-line, through alder and hazel woodland to the grassy slope of Castlefields in 100 metres. Descend into the view, towards the hamlet of Voxmoor, to a stile beside a patch of bulrushes in 250 metres.

3 Pass Beacon Lane Farm in 150 metres and continue straight ahead (N) along Beacon Lane. This cherty track joins a road in 600 metres.

4 Turn right (E) down to Voxmoor in 300 metres. Fork left after Manderlay, opposite the granary and post-box, along a lane which follows the stream for 250 metres.

5 Turn left (N) along Monument Road to 1893-dated Calway's Farm and Barn End in 200 metres. Then continue along the road to Legglands Cottage in 200 metres. Proceed uphill, listening out for traffic on the narrow section of lane, to Legglands in 150 metres.

6 Turn right (SE) along its drive, passing the house, to the kissing gate in 75 metres. Enter the field and pass the trees, notably an appropriate Wellingtonia commemorating the strategic wedding anniversaries of Michael and Yvonne Fox.

The iconic pillar.

Recovered from beside the quay at Exeter, the Georgian gun barrel is not fully authentic – being a naval cannon rather than an artillery piece – but the trunnion casting to Scottish maker 'Carron 1789' puts it in the right period.

Gun guard.

Wooded slopes.

> The National Trust owns 21 acres around the Wellington Monument and a further 61 acres of wild woodland at nearby Quarts Moor.

7 Descend to the stile between the holly bush and the oak tree, in the bottom right-hand corner of the field, in 250 metres. Proceed straight ahead across the stream at a footbridge in 50 metres. Then cross the stile in 100 metres. We are heading (S) towards the Blackdown Hills between Gortnell Common and Quarts Moor.

Autumn approach.

8 There is a large paddock to the left. Follow the wide grassy path fir 300 metres. Bear right across the stream at a concrete bridge and then turn left, for 150 metres, to the upper corner of a walled orchard. Continue straight ahead, following the back wall, to stiles and the road between Bidlands Cottage and Briscoe in another 150 metres.

The Iron Duke's door.

Somerset Wildlife Trust bought 25 acres of marshy grassland, along the spring-line at Castlefields – above Beacon Lane – in 1986.

9 Turn left (E) to pass the entrance to Briscoe House, and then right (S) in just 50 metres. Go up the lane to Quarts Farm in 300 metres. Here we continue straight ahead, between the cottage and the barn, as the farm road becomes a stony green lane. Follow it into the woodlands and up to the summit of the plateau in 1,100 metres.

10 Turn right (W) at a stile (about 150 metres before reaching the hilltop road) on to a National Trust path into Quarts Moor woods. Continue straight ahead across the car-park in 350 metres to a stile, to the right of the entrance, into the next block of woodland. Proceed to its far left-hand corner in 250 metres.

Plinth architecture.

11 Cross the stile beside the Trust's omega-shaped sign and turn right along the road to the cross-roads in 400 metres.

12 Continue straight ahead, passing Hemyock Place, to return to your car in 200 metres.

Top:
Quarts Moor.

Bottom:
Voxmoor.

Wrangway sheep.

3 Clayhidon and Simonsburrow

A 6.5-mile round walk through woods and valleys

The uplands of the northern line of the Blackdown Hills are interspersed with deep valleys. This exploration, via viewpoint slopes above Hemyock reaches the edge of the other escarpment, overlooking Taunton Deane, from the Wellington Monument. Contrasting with the great valley of the M5 and trading estates these hills are studded with wild woodland and rustic corners. Unimproved pastures are rich with wild flowers on a scale that is rare these days in the rural England of intensive agriculture.

Level: 🥾🥾🥾
Length: 6.5 miles
Terrain: Plenty of slopes with squelchy dips between.
Park & start: In Clayhidon village.
Start ref: ST 162 154
Postcode: EX15 3TJ
Public transport: Buses between Wellington and Hemyock.
Websites:
www.devon.gov.uk
www.nationaltrust.org.uk

This is an older countryside with a couple of relict tracts of common land which used to be scoured by the poor for fuel to keep their home fires burning. And throughout much of the route buzzards and deer are commonplace.

Map labels

Wellington Monument
10
11
8
Hemyock Place
Monument
12
Simons Burrow Farm
Simonsburrow
Heazle Farm
13
ASHCULME TURBARY
Jenning's Farm
Half Moon Inn
Clayhidon
CLAYHIDON TURBARY
1
Mount Pleasant Farm
2
Ashculme
3
7
4
Black Lane
suckle
age
6
5
Lower Ashculme Farm
Tanhouse Farm

Scale 500m

N W E S

1 Set off from the Half Moon Inn into the drive to St Andrew's Church and turn left (W) in 30 metres, into the bridleway beside the car-park. This brings us to a house in 200 metres and follows its drive to a lane in another 200 metres.

2 Turn left at the road and then right in 30 metres along the drive to Mount Pleasant Farm in 200 metres. Go down into the pasture, to the gate to the right of the old cottage in 75 metres, and enter the wild country of Clayhidon Turbary. Turn left (SW), up the slope, to the gate on to the road in 300 metres.

3 Turn right along Black Lane, downhill, to the junction in 800 metres.

4 Turn left (S) beside Tanhouse Farm and follow the valley stream to approach Lower Ashculme Farm in 200 metres.

Leaving the Half Moon.

Clayhidon Church.

Monument approach.

5   Turn right (NW) into a green lane and follow it up the hill. Continue straight ahead at the junction of tracks in 400 metres and then follow the side of Combe Hill around to the left (SW) in 100 metres, overlooking Hemyock.

The effigy of a vested priest in a canopy tomb in St Andrew's Church belonged to the family who gave the parish the second element of its name, and probably represents Ralph de Hidon, who died in 1273.

6   Continue straight ahead along the road in 250 metres. Turn right (N) at the next junction, in 200 metres, to pass Honeysuckle Cottage and other hillside homes with a view across to Dartmoor. Proceed ahead at Pen Cross junction in 600 metres. Continue uphill to the other side of the hillside wood at the corner in 250 metres.

7   Turn left here, at the stile and gate, and follow the hillside terrace with the wood stretching down to the left and fields over the hedge to the right. Keep following the upper hedgerow through the woods and across a couple of pastures above Grey Walls, to a third and final pasture in 1,500 metres. Walk across this field to the gate and stile in the corner, in 100 metres, below roadside beech trees.

8   Turn left (W) along the road, downhill around the corner beside Monument Farm in 150 metres, and proceed for a further 300 metres.

9   Turn right (N) along a green lane, to a gate across it, in 150 metres. Turn right (NE), through the gate into the woods, beside a National Trust sign. Follow the

Ashculme.

Clayhidon Turbary.

boundary bank straight ahead for 600 metres and then turn right (S), up the escarpment, to the Wellington Monument in 150 metres.

10 Leave the Monument by crossing the plateau grassland (SE), to the main access drive beside Firs Plantation, and the car-park in 800 metres.

Ashculme Turbary and matching moorland on the other side of the valley at Clayhidon Turbary take their names from the use of peaty turves as fuel by the peasantry who also gathered 'estovers' of gorse-faggots and kindling wood.

Japanese rhubarb.

11 Turn left (E) along the road beside Hemyock Place — ensuring you face oncoming traffic — to the cross-roads in 150 metres.

12 Turn right (S) to Simons Burrow Farm in 500 metres. Continue for a further 300 metres and then turn left (E) in Simonsburrow hamlet beside the Old Chapel. Descend the steep slope and enter Ashculme

> *Clayhidon parish sprawls across more than seven square miles of sparsely populated countryside and has a second inn — the Merrier Harriers — at Forches Corner on the main road beside the northern escarpment.*

Rustic gates.

Turbary, beside Flints, in 100 metres. Stay on the bridleway into the woodland beyond in 100 metres. Pass farmsteads above the valley ponds in 600 metres and climb up to Jenning's Farm and the road in a further 500 metres.

Grey Walls orchids.

Beech-lined bank.

Honeysuckle Cottage.

13 Turn left (N) to pass a wood and approach Higher Heazle after the corner in 600 metres. Turn right here (E) and right again in 100 metres. Bear left and then right after the stables in 50 metres.

Follow the hedgerow, keeping it to your right, and enter a leafy green lane in 400 metres.

This brings us to the wall beside the Old Rectory into Clayhidon village in 300 metres.

Pen Cross.

4 **Churchstanton and Stapley**

A strenuous 6-mile circuit through the damp and lush heartlands of these hills

Level: 🥾 🥾 🥾

Length: 6 miles

Terrain: Soggy and stony into the valleys.

Park & start: In Churchstanton, in the car-park opposite the parish church of St Peter and St Paul.

Start ref: ST 196 145

Postcode: TA3 7QE

Public transport: None

Websites:
www.tauntondeane.gov.uk
www.ukvillages.co.uk.

The core highlands of the Blackdown Hills are only intermittently inhabited. There is a plentiful spread of small farmsteads but they give the impression of having been recently cleared from a forest that still exists. It is a convincing illusion. Pause on a hilltop and scan the view for 180 degrees. In most places the skyline treetops will be an unbroken one hundred per cent of the view. As for conditions underfoot, expect mud and stones, and the lush vegetation that comes with hills that are often under a cloud. Chert beds and greensand sit on a bed of clay which means that the spring-line is the norm across a patchwork of little fields and long escarpments.

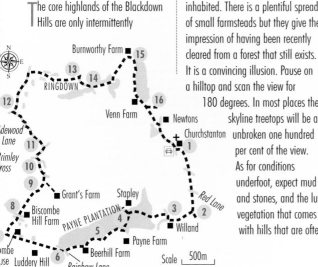

Burnworthy Farm ■ 15
13
14
RINGDOWN
12
Venn Farm ■ 16
■ Newtons
✝ Churchstanton
🚗 1
dewood Lane
11
rimley oss
10
9
■ Grant's Farm   Stapley   *Red Lane*
8
Biscombe   3
Hill Farm   4   2
PAYNE PLANTATION
5   ■ Willand
mbe se   6
Luddery Hill   ■ Beerhill Farm
Farm   *Rainbow Lane*   ■ Payne Farm
Scale 500m

Churchstanton Church.

1 Set off along Church Road (S) for 50 metres and pass the drive to Churchstanton House which used to be the Rectory. Turn left into the next entrance. Bear right across the pasture, diagonally, to the stile between beech and sycamore trees near the corner. Follow the hedge straight ahead to the gate in 400 metres. Cross Church Road, into the wide droveway, and also cross Red Lane in 300 metres.

2 Turn right in 350 metres into a narrow double-banked track (W) to Willand in 400 metres.

3 Turn right on reaching the lane and then left across a stile. Follow the hedgerow straight ahead, crossing holly bush stiles. Enter woodland in 250 metres. Cross footbridges and join a path between ivy-clad stone walls into Stapley hamlet in 350 metres.

4 Turn left (S), crossing the ford, up a double-banked track through Paye Plantation. Briefly leave the woodland as you approach Paye Farm in 350 metres. Then turn sharply right (W) along a second path. Keep the wood to your right and fields to the left for 700 metres.

5 Pass Beerhill Farm, keeping its buildings to your left for 100 metres, and turn right beside an old pond at the far corner of the last barn. Walk the length of the pasture to Rainbow Lane in 350 metres.

6 Cross to the stile and follow the hedge with Luddery Hill Farm on the other side in 250 metres. Enter the left-hand corner of the wood in 150 metres and follow its upper boundary. Cross the grassy grounds of Biscombe House in 500 metres.

7 Turn right (NE) on reaching the beech trees. Follow the trees down to the drive and exit from this orchid-rich parkland at the gates opposite a pillar box in 300 metres.

Rebuilt in 1830, with a crude gargoyle reset in the tower, St Peter and St Paul's Church at Churchstanton retains a 1625-dated oak bier, and the parish stocks.

Oak and stump.

8 Cross the road to the field gate to the left of Biscombe Hill Farm. Follow the hedgerow for 400 metres down to the bottom right-hand part of the pasture, to a stile 35 metres from the corner. Turn right and then left. Cross this field diagonally to a gate and monastic stepping stones across a stream in 175 metres. The right-hand woody hedge leads uphill to a thatched cottage above Grants Farm.

9 Cross the stile after the power cables at the top of the field in 250 metres. Follow the track uphill to the road in 200 metres.

10 Turn left, down to the bungalow and junction at Brimley Cross in 350 metres. Turn right, downhill, to the next junction in 250 metres.

Brimley Hill thatch.

Grant's Farm stepping stones.

11 Turn left (NW) down Hidewood Lane. Cross the River Culm and continue straight at the junction in 500 metres. Bear right (N) beside the house in 300 metres into Applehayes Lane.